My Faith and Courage

Georgann Dolin Hendren

AuthorHouse™
1663 Liberty Drive, Suite 200
Bloomington, IN 47403
www.authorhouse.com
Phone: 1-800-839-8640

© *2007 Georgann Dolin Hendren. All rights reserved.*

No part of this book may be reproduced, stored in a retrieval system, or transmitted by any means without the written permission of the author.

First published by AuthorHouse 12/27/2007

ISBN: 978-1-4343-5117-3 (sc)

Library of Congress Control Number: 2007909510

Printed in the United States of America
Bloomington, Indiana

This book is printed on acid-free paper.

"For A Day of My Life" poem by Samuel F. Pugh

Cover: Dick, Katie and Richard Hendren
Composite photo of:
    46th Street   and   Figure Eight Island
    Virginia Beach, Virginia   Wilmington, North Carolina

Contact the author at: myfaithandcourage@yahoo.com

My Faith and Courage is the story of Georgann Dolin Hendren and her family. It follows Georgann through the trials and tribulations encountered during life-altering experiences. It shares the joys and triumphs of both her and her children. Her inspirational words will touch those who have faced the loss of a spouse or loved one and are seeking to work through the pain of their loss.

My Faith and Courage – Georgann's faith and courage – is a testament to one woman's strength and fortitude and her undying love of family.

DEDICATION

This book is dedicated to my two wonderful children, Katie Ann and Richard, who with their unconditional love gave me the strength, the courage and the will to move forward after the sudden death of their father, my husband and best friend. I love you Katie and Richard and I am so proud of both of you.

I am also dedicating this book to my parents, George and Margie Dolin, who would not let me give up on life as much as I wanted to. Their never-ending love and support helped me through my darkest days. Those days are in the past. I am so blessed to have you in my life. I love you Mom and Dad.

A heartfelt thanks to Merry J. Wieland for the countless hours she spent helping me get *My Faith and Courage* ready to publish. I would also like to thank everyone else who helped make this book a reality.

*Love,
Georgann*

Contents

The beginning....................................5

Born of the Spirit..............................17

Faith in the midst of tragedy.............21

As you trust in HIM..........................33

For when your faith is tested.............39

HIS unfailing love.............................45

A new life..51

HIS plan..65

Your body is the temple....................77

HIS peace will guard your hearts.......83

My faith and courage........................93

✝

Except for the 23rd Psalm, all biblical quotations in this book come from the Life Application Study Bible, New Living Translation, Copyright ©1996.

With death, there is life. A new life for the loved ones left behind. A new way of living each day. A new way of looking toward the future. New challenges, new direction. You dig deep inside to find the courage to move forward. This is not a better life, just different. You can choose to live like your loved one would want you to, or you can collapse from the grief that consumes your every waking moment.

I asked God why this had to happen to us. I was so angry with Him. I was very close to shutting the door on my faith, but God would not let me. He knew my pain and gently guided me through each day until I fully understood that God does good things through tragedy.

My husband's spirit is everywhere -- our church, the golf course we passed each day, and on the roads we traveled together, just to name a few. He has not been with me to physically share in high school, college, and boot camp graduations. He was not there when our son joined the Navy, and received his pilot's license. He missed his daughter's graduation from college and her first day of teaching. He missed helping me teach two teenagers how to drive a car, build a new home and survive a brain hemorrhage. Life experiences are now different because we are no longer sharing them with the one person who was so strong, loving and caring.

For a mother who was not a leader but a follower, it was difficult becoming "head of household" as the IRS classified me, but I did it. We did it stumbling along the way, depending on God, our church, family, and friends to help us through. I, along with my children, have chosen to live. It took several years to find that desire, but we are there now, successfully moving forward without a husband and a father to protect us from life's struggles and to share in all of our wonderful accomplishments. We want others who have lost a loved one to know there is hope for the future. With God all things are possible. Our names are Georgann, Katie, and Richard Hendren, and this is our story.

The Beginning

✝

Dick Hendren and I met in March of 1978. It was God's plan for us to meet. I wanted to move from St. Albans, West Virginia to Columbus, Ohio for no other reason than that friends told me it was a great place to live. I had already lived in several other cities since college but had not found a city in which I wanted to settle down. I was more of a free spirit who did not take life too seriously. My life had everything but direction. I was blessed with a wonderful family who let me fumble along the way as I tried making it on my own. They were always there to pick me up after I'd fallen.

I was working retail management and wanted a change -- my usual attitude when I became bored with life or work. I was now ready to settle down and wanted to find a more 9-5 routine. Retail hours are not the best and I became quite tired of always working nights and weekends. I decided to visit friends Sandy and Steve, who were temporarily living in Lancaster, Ohio, about 30 miles south of Columbus. Sandy and I met at Greenbrier School For Girls in Lewisburg, West Virginia back in the 60's and had remained good friends since that time. She was married to Steve and Steve's job had transferred them to Lancaster from Charleston, West Virginia.

I began the tedious task of job hunting by checking the classified section of the Columbus Dispatch. I responded to an advertisement which was listed through an employment agency. Hoping to schedule an interview for that afternoon, I called the number listed in the paper but was disconnected before I could complete my conversation with the receptionist. I returned the call and once again we were disconnected. I was about to give up but something prompted me to try one more time. The third attempt was a success. I spoke to a counselor and the appointment was made for an interview late that afternoon.

Driving from Lancaster to Columbus took much longer than I planned and getting lost did not help. I was very late arriving for the interview, and I had second thoughts of even going into the office building, but something told me to continue on with this venture. I entered the empty lobby to find a woman standing in the doorway of her small office. Her attention was directed toward me as I walked through the lobby door. I instantly assumed she was the person with whom I would be interviewing. She said, "You must be Georgann. We have been waiting for you." No one had cell phones in those days so there was no way for me to call and explain I was running late. We shook hands as I apologized profusely. She was understanding but I could sense that she was interested in getting the interview started. I handed her a copy of my resume, as she asked me to fill out an application for employment. After that process was complete, she informed me that I needed to interview with the office manager and to please follow her to his office. I followed her back to the last office at the end of the hallway to find a gentleman sitting behind a cluttered desk. He rose from his chair and as we were being introduced, he politely shook my hand. His name was Dick Hendren.

After the interview, Dick Hendren offered me a position with the company as a new recruiter. It wasn't the job for which I was applying, but I thought I should accept this opportunity. I wanted to get to know this man better. I was really not interested in the job at all. He explained I would need to be trained for the position since

I lacked experience in this field. He said it would take the rest of the week and asked if I could start training tomorrow afternoon. I said yes, the time was set, and we said our goodbyes as he escorted me to the lobby door. I had an instant attraction to this man. We just clicked. I knew it was the only reason I accepted the job offer in the first place. He had a great personality and an attraction I could not explain. I was intrigued by his confidence and charisma. I knew I wanted to get to know him better and the best way to do that, I thought, was to work for him. I was sure I had just met the man I was going to marry. I assumed he was single because he wasn't wearing a wedding ring.

At the time, I knew little about him personally, but I was giddy with excitement as I drove the thirty miles back to Lancaster. I rushed into Sandy and Steve's apartment to tell them the good news. I explained about finding a job, but, more importantly, I let them know that I had met the man I was going to marry. They were excited about my first comment about finding a job but chuckled at the second remark – about me finding a husband as well. As I began to tell them more about this man I had just met, the conversation became less about the job I had just accepted. You could tell by the look on their faces that they thought I was being rather presumptuous about finding my future husband. I made plans to stay with them for a few more days while I looked for an apartment in Columbus.

I was on time for training the next afternoon. The next several days were spent reading text, taking notes and learning all aspects of a recruiter's job. I was anxious to get settled in my own apartment. Throughout the process, I was becoming more interested in Dick, and I could tell he was becoming interested in me. It was late Friday afternoon and we were ending our training sessions for the weekend. I was preparing to begin interviewing clients on Monday morning. Dick asked if I would like to have dinner to celebrate. Of course I said yes. It was all I could do to remain cool as I accepted his invitation. Our dinner conversation led us to openly admit we were interested in dating each other. We discussed that it was not a good idea to date since we would be working together and especially since he was my boss. I suggested I could find another job, not being real sure what that might be. I was taking a chance leaving this job before it started, but I knew I really had no other options if I wanted to pursue a personal relationship with him.

On Monday I told the president of the company I could not start work due to personal reasons. He was furious with me since they had wasted an entire week training me. I soon found another job in retail and within a couple of months of dating each other, Dick and I were discussing marriage. We had fallen in love. Dick and I were engaged that Christmas and married on April 28, 1979. It was God's plan for us to meet.

We lived in Columbus where I was working downtown for the landmark Lazarus Department Store. I became friends with a co-worker named Julie. She was younger than me and worked part-time at Lazarus while completing her bachelor's degree at Ohio State University. We spoke often and I soon realized she would be a good match for my younger brother Robert. I was playing matchmaker as I told each of them they should meet. Robert was attending Marshall University in Huntington, West Virginia and explained he would try to make a trip to Columbus soon. I gave Robert Julie's phone number and left the rest to them. Robert visited Dick and I one weekend and he and Julie met for the first time. Within a few months, they were dating and becoming very interested in each other. I watched as their relationship matured. I was happy for both of them as I watched them become closer. They were married several years later and are now the proud parents of four boys and live in Boston, Massachusetts.

If I had not quit the job at my husband's office and found the new job at Lazarus, my brother Robert and sister-in-law Julie would not be married today. We don't realize that God is working His plan for us while we are busy living our lives. Sometimes we just need to stop and listen for His direction. He will guide us through each day in unexpected ways. I am sure you can think of something that has happened in your life where God was working His plan for you. You just didn't realize it at that exact moment.

Dick and I were both from large families. When we married, my parents George and Margie had their primary residence in St. Albans, West Virginia. My sister Nancy, her husband Buddy, and Nancy's identical twin Libby were living in Raleigh N.C. My brother David was living in Norfolk, Virginia and attending Old Dominion College. Robert and Julie were living in Columbus at the time. Dick's family all lived in Virginia Beach -- Pat and L.P. (Dick's mom and step-dad), Dick Sr. and step-mother Claudia, sisters Vicki, Wanda, and Terry, and step-siblings Larry and Dee Dee. Having large families, we always enjoyed sharing time together. We looked forward to our visits to Virginia Beach and Snowshoe Mountain in West Virginia where my parents had a second home. We had the best of both worlds -- the beach in the summer and snow skiing in the winter.

My biological clock was ticking as they say, but when we found out we were expecting in August, we were rather surprised. Dick was so anxious to find out if we were pregnant that he called for the results of the pregnancy test before I could make the call to the lab. He actually gave me the good news over the phone. Katherine Ann Hendren was born April 18th, 1980. She was our pride and joy; she was daddy's little girl. Life was very good and we felt very blessed. Katie brought so much joy to our life.

We wanted more children and learned fifteen months later we were expecting our second child in February, 1982. My pregnancy was normal, but for some reason unknown to my doctors, Richard Robert Hendren III was born six weeks premature on December 19th, 1981. His dad and I rejoiced that we had a son, but the jubilation was overshadowed by the concern for our son's serious health issues. Richard's complications were few, but serious enough for him to stay in the neo-natal special care unit for the next twelve days. My parents helped by taking Katie home with them to West Virginia. This was a Christmas we would never forget. We brought Richard home from the hospital on New Year's Eve. My parents brought

Katie back home to us on New Year's Day and we celebrated the new year being thankful for our precious children. Life was complete. We had a solid marriage and two beautiful children who were active and healthy. We dearly loved our family and always looked forward to our time together.

Dick and I discussed religion before we were married. We occasionally attended church, but we were not actively serving God. The years passed quickly as we tried to make it through life without Christ. Dick had a massive heart attack on March 17, 1987. He was rushed to the hospital where the diagnosis was critical. I was so afraid I was going to lose my husband. I reached out for Christ to help me get through this frightening time. I did not give it any thought that we were not active followers of Christ and maybe He would not hear my prayers or cries. Our Christian upbringing gave us a good foundation for understanding that Christ loves us unconditionally and His Grace is given to us whether we deserve it or not.

After several weeks in the cardiac intensive care unit, Dick was well enough to continue his recuperation at home. The children were too young to understand that their father had survived a massive heart attack. At the age of 6 and 7, they were just excited to have him home. He soon returned to a full schedule, working, playing sports, and doing about anything he chose. We prayed, giving thanks for God's healing. Our intentions of learning more about God's word became sidelined by our busy life. We wasted valuable time trying to make it on our own, not relying on God to guide us through each day. We made a lot of mistakes, trying to live life on our own. It would take many more years for us to realize that something was missing in our life. That something was not having a solid relationship with Christ.

I was a stay-at-home mom for several years. I enjoyed taking care of our children and our home. I was constantly working on small projects. Everyone knew that I was not afraid to tackle anything. I soon began to ask Dick for power tools and he purchased them for me. My family and friends found it a bit unconventional for me to

My Faith and Courage

receive the newest Black and Decker hand tool for Christmas, but Dick knew it was what I really wanted.

A few years later, out of necessity, I started looking for a part-time job. For several years, I had volunteered in the children's elementary school and enjoyed working with children. When I saw an ad in the paper for an assistant site director for the Worthington Care After School program, I became excited about the prospects of working for them. I interviewed with the program coordinators and was hired in June of 1990. My job would begin in August when school was back in session. Little did I know how that job would contribute to my ability to face my future challenges -- but God knew. He was working His plan.

While in the third grade, our daughter, Katie, was diagnosed with a learning disability. The teachers and her father and I watched over her academics closely. She was finding school to be very difficult, and by the time she was ready to begin the sixth grade, we knew she needed more than what the public school system could provide. We researched private education and found a school that met all of Katie's academic and social needs. Marburn Academy in Columbus not only taught a full academic curriculum but also taught Katie techniques she could use to achieve her goals of becoming confident in all areas of her life. The school specialized in working with students who learned differently. They did not convey the learning difference as a disability. Katie became so driven that nothing became impossible for her as she gained academic success and confidence. Her first year at Marburn reinforced her plan to become a teacher. She became excited about school and learning. Thank you, Marburn, for giving my daughter the tools and confidence to achieve her goals.

Richard did not have a problem with academics, but applying himself was another matter as he continued in the public system. As an intellectual, he was always thinking and wanting to learn more about subjects he was interested in and not necessarily the academics he needed to focus on. I am glad that he has such an inquisitive mind, always analyzing everything. Unfortunately, that would hinder his ability to find most of the school curriculum interesting and to become academically successful as he continued with his education. He had trouble focusing on the task at hand, which was graduating from high school and hopefully going on to college. Richard is quick to admit that he did not always apply himself during middle and high school. He looks back and now sees the importance of being committed to a higher standard of learning.

Dick was a member of the Westerville Lions Club and enjoyed the community service opportunities that came with being a member of that club. He joined shortly after we were married. He gave 100% at both the state and national level. He enjoyed the friendship and comradery the members shared. I thank them for their genuine friendship. Along with his fellow club members, Dick was a sports enthusiast. He loved all sports and played on several different teams/leagues throughout our married life. Dick's favorite, though, was golf. He played golf throughout middle and high school and I was the typical golf widow. I look back and realize being a golf widow was not so terrible. He enjoyed every moment he was on the golf course. The Lions Club had a group of men who formed a Thursday golf league at Tablerock Golf Course, thirty miles north of Columbus in Centerburg.

Dick and I had a strong desire to leave the hectic city for the quiet life in the country, yet we needed to choose a location within a reasonable proximity to our jobs. I was promoted to site director with the understanding I would be able to get to work easily from wherever we chose to live. Commuting with snow and ice on the roads during winter months had to be taken into consideration. I was currently registered to return to college to complete the necessary course work the state required of me to be a director for an after school program. I did not want my commute to become difficult and exhausting as the years progressed.

By this time, Dick was golfing at Tablerock Golf Course a couple times a week, sometimes more, so he had the opportunity to learn a little about the small community of Centerburg. He thought we should check it out as a place to live as soon as possible. I had never been to Centerburg, so I was interested to see where he golfed and just what this rural area had to offer. We drove the miles of country roads for a couple of hours and fell in love with the peaceful scenic landscape. We discussed our future on the quiet drive to Knox County. Could we possibly live here? Would this be the place we would retire and live comfortably the rest of our lives?

We returned home to discuss with Katie and Richard our desire to move to the country. Katie and Richard have always been very close and share things that only siblings can. Richard dislikes change, so he was not as anxious to leave the only home and neighborhood he had ever known. We tried to ease his concerns, but knew he would have reservations about moving. Katie had an easier time accepting the planned change. The usual anxiety of moving was evident, but she adjusted much better than Richard.

After several months we sold our house, and in June of 1995 we planned our move to Centerburg, the geographical center of Ohio. Since we wanted to take our time to find the right piece of property to build our new home, we decided to put most of our furniture in storage and rent a small apartment in the village. A few days before the move, Dick was in Centerburg checking on our apartment when he stopped by the Hometown Market, our local IGA grocery store. A church youth group was having a car wash. Dick loved a clean car, so when he was asked if he wanted his car washed he could not resist. After all, it was a fund raiser for some youth group for some local church.

Jay and Karen, our next door neighbors for many years in Columbus, had moved to Centerburg the previous year with their four children. Our friendship continued as we made plans to move close to where they were living. God put Karen and Jay in our lives not only to be lasting friends, but for Karen to eventually be instrumental in saving my life a few years later. Karen told us about the Centerburg United Methodist Church and that we should attend a worship service once we were moved. Her family was already actively involved in the church.

I know God was working His plan because while the youth were washing Dick's car, he and a gentleman engaged in a brief discussion about us moving to Centerburg in a few days. The man ended the conversation by telling Dick that his name was Mark Coale and he was the pastor of the Centerburg United Methodist Church. He invited us to a Sunday worship service. Dick was giving the youth a donation when he turned to tell Mark we would definitely be at church as soon as we were moved.

Dick drove away with a sparkling car and returned home to Columbus. He shared with me the events of his afternoon car wash. He explained about meeting the minister of Karen's church and how much he enjoyed their conversation. He expressed a strong desire to attend Sunday worship service as soon as we moved, which was scheduled for the next week. It gives me chills as I look back on how God was working His plan. I said with a sigh, "Yes, we will go", thinking how exhausted I would be. My husband was so excited about the prospect of finding a church with which he felt comfortable. I was not going to disappoint him.

"Just as you can hear the wind but can't tell where it comes from or where it's going, so you can't explain how people are born of the Spirit."

John 3:8

†

It was a warm Sunday morning in June. Exhausted by the move, we made our way to church. We were greeted by several people when Mark approached to welcome us. We found a seat in this small, crowded, one hundred year old country church. The rich wood tone of the pews and alter revealed the years of service this church had given. I wanted to learn more about the history. I looked around to see the deep maroon carpet typical of most churches I had attended. The congregation was engaging in a soft social conversation. Who are these people? I wondered. Several people glanced our way and said welcome. "Nice", I thought, as I sat in silence. The sun glistened through the most beautiful stained glass windows I had ever seen. We were overwhelmed by what we felt. I was a little distracted from the sermon as I sat next to Dick wondering if he was feeling the same thing I was feeling. Was this going to become our church?

After the service, as we were preparing to leave the sanctuary, we were greeted by more church members with such a welcoming spirit. We left the church feeling very good, but I was cautious. I thought how could there be so many loving and caring people in one place, even if it was God's house. Dick was excited. We were both thirsting for God to be in our lives.

Our lives actually changed that day. We both felt it. "Just as you can hear the wind but can't tell where it comes from or where it's going, so you can't explain how people are born of the Spirit." John 3:8. A peace and contentment came over us. We became active, almost immediately, in the Centerburg United Methodist Church. Serving God became a priority for us. We were no longer content with occasionally attending a Sunday worship service. We wanted to contribute to the ministry of Jesus Christ and what better way to begin than through our fellowship with our church family. Our marriage became stronger. We were walking in a newness of life. We were transformed. Our friends noticed a dramatic change in both of us. How exciting to experience a rebirth in Christ! Dick actually stopped golfing on Sundays. The Sabbath became the day God intended. It was reserved for church and family. Dick, Katie and I became members of the Centerburg United Methodist Church on November 19, 1995. Our son Richard would join in membership later.

Faith in the midst of tragedy

†

I had no idea what God had planned for us fifteen months later, but God knew. Jesus said to them "you don't need to know the time of those events that only the Father controls." Acts1:7. I thank God for those wonderful months and memories I will forever cherish.

Our children's first experience with the death of a family member came when Dick's father suddenly passed away on December 10th, 1995. Our children were inquisitive about the death and burial process, and the planning of a funeral. We answered their questions as best we could. It was the first time they watched their father weep with sorrow. He had lost a best friend and grieved deeply. The hymn *Amazing Grace* impacted their hearts as they heard it being sung. That song would eventually impact their very soul many months later. We reflected on a father's and grandfather's love and how he would be sadly missed. We returned to Centerburg with a quiet sadness, knowing our trips to Virginia Beach would forever change.

On February fourth, Dick became ill. We did not know what was wrong but we knew we needed to get him to the hospital. He was in an incredible amount of pain. It was heartbreaking watching him suffer. When the diagnosis of cryptococcal meningitis was finally made, the doctors wanted to get Dick settled into ICU. It was now close to 6:00 P.M. and would take a while before we could see him again.

I needed to control my emotions as the diagnosis was being explained to me. Richard was listening to every word. I did not have to say much, but he could tell by the look on my face that this was very serious. Unfortunately, I still did not fully understand what meningitis was and knew very little about the disease. I did know that I needed to get Katie to the hospital, since she was at home anxiously waiting for news about her father. It was important for the three of us to be together. We lived an hour from the hospital and Katie and Richard did not drive. What was I going to do? I needed to start making phone calls. Family and friends were waiting to hear what was happening. I needed to call our minister Mark, Dick's parents, my parents. I was reliving Dick's heart attack all over again. I knew everyone had been concerned about Dick these past couple of weeks because he was not feeling well.

I decided to call our friend Karen. She had visited us at home the night before and was adamant about wanting to help if I needed her. I explained the situation and asked if she would please pick up Katie and bring her to the hospital. I felt like I was asking for the world because we lived so far away and it was late, but Karen did not hesitate. She was a paramedic for the Centerburg emergency squad and when I told her the diagnosis was cryptococcal meningitis, she knew that it was not good. She told me she would be at the hospital with Katie as soon as she safely could. I called our minister, Mark. He also did not hesitate to say he was on his way.

I was very grateful to both of them as I prayed to God for strength. He answered my prayer. "He gives power to those who are tired and worn out; he offers strength to the weak." Isaiah 40:29. I still had several phone calls to make, but I did have a renewed strength. I put my plan in motion to take charge and deal with the complexity of what we were facing. I called the family one at a time to express my concerns and convey the recent diagnosis of meningitis. Pat and LP

My Faith and Courage

made plans to arrive as soon as they could get to Columbus from Virginia Beach, and my parents were on their way from Snowshoe, West Virginia. I called Dick's very good friends Kingston and Don. The word spread quickly that the diagnosis was meningitis. Prayers began as Richard and I sat in the cold, dimly lit waiting room, watching for Katie, Karen and Mark to arrive and for some encouraging word from the doctors.

Richard and I were told we could see Dick although we could not stay in his room long. We walked into ICU to see him hooked up to so many machines. I was nervous for Richard to see his father like this. I was reminded of the time he was hospitalized from his heart attack and the machines he was connected to ten years ago. One is never prepared to see a loved one dependent on so many machines. He was incoherent and had to be restrained because he kept pulling the tubes from his arm. Richard was upset about his dad being restrained, and he did not understand why it was a necessity. Richard tried to comfort his father by softly telling him everything was going to be ok and that we were there with him. Of course he did not respond. I was nervously asking the nurses questions about his care.

It was soon time for us to leave Dick's bedside and return to the waiting room to wait for Katie, Karen and Mark to arrive. Richard and I sat motionless as we reflected back on the day and what was happening. It was hard to comprehend that my husband was fighting for his life. Katie and Karen arrived with Mark close behind. I tried to explain to them what I knew. Richard was relieved to see his sister. It was comforting to have her there with us. The three of us stood there consoling each other. Little did we know that our lives as we knew them had changed forever. We could not prepare ourselves for what was going to happen. Mark said a prayer and then asked if he could see Dick. I said of course. I could see the concern in both Karen's and Mark's eyes. They knew the seriousness of the diagnosis of meningitis. I was oblivious to how this insidious disease was consuming his brain. Karen suggested we go home and get some much needed rest. We could return early in the morning to resume our vigil at the hospital. I did not want to leave but was convinced it would be best for Katie and Richard, too.

Going home gave me a few hours to arrange a leave of absence from my job and for Katie and Richard to be out of school indefinitely. We each packed clothes for several days and tried to rest between phone calls to the hospital to check on Dick's condition. Katie, Richard and I returned to the hospital very early the next morning.

My brother David and sister-in-law Sue, who live in California, realized how far we lived from the hospital and called me to suggest we consider moving to the closest hotel so we could spend as much time as we needed at the hospital. I agreed and they took care of everything. I was so grateful. Pat and L.P., Dick's parents, his sister Wanda, and my parents, George and Margie arrived early that afternoon. We took turns checking into the hotel. Since we did not want to leave Dick alone, we decided to take shifts staying at the hospital so we could each get a little rest. The volunteer in the ICU waiting room kept fielding calls from all over the United States concerning Dick's condition. It was overwhelming for us to witness the outpouring of love from everyone. We were comforted knowing prayers were being said for each of us. God was helping us through each difficult moment and each difficult decision. Our church family was keeping vigil from Centerburg. It was also comforting to know they were prepared to help in any way they could.

After several days, we were told that the medicine was not working. There had been many complications. Dick had been placed on life support several days earlier. We stood helplessly by as we were told he was not going to make it. I was asked to make a decision about when to remove the respirator. I thought how can I possibly make such a decision? I told the doctors that I would let them know tomorrow. I just kept repeating myself, "tomorrow, tomorrow, tomorrow." I was about to collapse from exhaustion when I was taken to the hotel to get some much needed rest. I did not want to leave the hospital. In the cold, dark hotel room I cried out to God to help me with the decision I was asked to make. I tried to rationalize why Dick was

My Faith and Courage

not going to die and how he was going to pull through, although in my heart I knew the truth. I fell asleep crying, begging God for a miracle.

It was early morning when I was awakened by a knock at my hotel door. I could not believe it was daylight. I only planned to sleep for a short while and return back to Dick's room. It was my mother telling me the hospital had just called. We had been asked to return to the hospital immediately. Dick was slipping away. It was not going to be long. The hotel had gotten our room numbers mixed up. Instead of putting the hospital through to my hotel room, they were connected to my parent's room. My mother decided to break the news to me instead of letting the hospital do it.

I called the family together as we quickly prepared for the short drive back to the hospital. Everything was moving in slow motion. It was like a bad dream from which I wanted desperately to awaken. My husband was not dying. This was all a terrible mistake.

Katie, Richard, my mother and I quietly slipped into the car as my dad sped away to the front door of the hospital. We left the car in the no-parking zone and rushed through the doors. It was so early that the lobby was quiet and only the custodian emptying the trash cans took notice of us. The rest of the family followed close behind – Pat, LP and Wanda. We held each other as we hurriedly walked through the hospital lobby onto the elevator. I did not know how to comfort my children or what to say. They were old enough to know what was happening. The elevator stopped on the 11th floor. My heart was pounding. I remember not wanting to step off the elevator. I thought if I stay on that elevator, time would stop, and I would not have to face the fact that my husband was dying. I was jolted back to reality as I looked at my children's faces. They were depending on me to be strong, and that was what I was going to do.

I took a deep breath as I stepped off the elevator and walked into ICU. It was like we were the only family in that hospital unit. Katie, Richard and I walked directly to Dick's room. We were met by the nurse and doctor on duty. The monitors indicated what the doctors had already confirmed. They explained that his organs were shutting down. It would not be long now. I raised my voice with an urgency for them to remove the tape from his eyes, and to remove the respirator. It was a decision I made without hesitation. The anguish I had a few hours earlier relating to the time I would give permission to remove my husband's life support was made for me. The time was now. My husband was dying and I could not do anything about it. I did not want to prolong his suffering.

We were asked to leave for a moment while they removed the respirator and in all reality prepared Dick to die. We reluctantly obliged as we stepped right outside the ICU doors. I explained to the family who were waiting in the hallway that we would be able to join together around Dick's bed in a few moments. I don't remember calling Mark, our minister, but he was there. I was so grateful to have him with us as we were escorted back to Dick's bedside. We stepped into the dimly lit, sterile hospital room. There was an eerie silence as I looked at my dear husband lying so peacefully in his hospital bed. I noticed the sun shining through his tiny intensive care unit window, casting a bright ray of sunshine on his still body. There were no more machines except the silent heart monitor turned from our view. We softly wiped the tears from our eyes as his breath became more shallow. Holding his hands, we surrounded his bed. Mark stood at the foot of my husband's bed and began reading Psalm 23:

> The Lord is my Shepherd; I shall not want.
>
> He maketh me to lie down in green pastures;
>
> He leadeth me beside the still waters.
>
> He restoreth my soul.
>
> He leadeth me in the paths of righteousness for his name's sake.
>
> Yea, though I walk through the valley of the shadow of death, I

will fear no evil;

For thou art with me; thy rod and thy staff they comfort me.

Thou preparest a table before me in the presence of mine enemies;

Thou anointest my head with oil; my cup runneth over.

Surely goodness and mercy shall follow me all the days of my life:

And I will dwell in the house of the Lord forever.

I could feel God's presence. Dick was finally at peace. It was evident to each of us as we tearfully recited the Lord's Prayer. The nurse standing with us had tears in her eyes too, as we watched Dick take his last breath. Death is frightening. It casts a shadow over us as we are helpless to stop it. It has the final word. There were no sad goodbyes from Dick. We did not get to tell him how much we loved him. He never knew what his frail body was battling. He was now at peace. Only the loved ones left behind were struggling with letting him go. Richard Robert Hendren, Jr. passed away February 26th 1997. He died with grace and dignity.

We left the hospital in silence the same way we entered, only this time I was hurt by the lack of sympathy from people continuing on with their lives as they rushed through the hospital lobby. Didn't they know that my husband had just died and that my heart was breaking? Of course they didn't. How could they? I wanted to scream out and let the world know. I wanted to be alone with my children. I wanted to go to sleep and never wake up. I wanted to die.

What I wanted to do and what I had to do were two different things. I was unfamiliar with what to do next. I had never planned a funeral before. I relied on our good friend Kingston to help me make final arrangements with the funeral home. Kingston and Don were very close friends of my husband and were there to help me through this most difficult time. There were so many decisions that needed to be made. My children were reluctant to agree on the solo hymn

Amazing Grace, which would be sung by Susie our choir director. They thought maybe we should choose a different song. They had been impacted by the words of the song after their grandfather's death and knew it would be a constant reminder of their father's funeral as well. Although the decision was difficult, we agreed we wanted the song included. It's a song Katie still has difficulty listening to without shedding a tear.

The funeral home and Pat, LP, Wanda, and Vicki helped me write the obituary and prepare for visitation, and our minister, Mark helped me plan the funeral and explain cremation to my children. I relied on Dick's parents and sisters for strength and direction. I will never forget gathering the items of clothing for the funeral home. Pat, Vicki, Wanda and I walked into my house after not being there for several weeks. I felt an emptiness, a loneliness, knowing my husband was never going to walk through this house again. Pat and I entered our bedroom to find his shoes tucked neatly at the foot of the bed where he took them off the night before we left for the hospital. His watch was lying on our dresser. The silent gripping pain in my chest would not go away. I knew Pat, Vicki, and Wanda's hearts were breaking, too, as we chose a white dress shirt and favorite tie. Pat was burying her only son. Vicki and Wanda were saying goodbye to their brother. I would need to prepare my children for the quiet loneliness that would surround us each and every moment we were in that house. How were we going to live without him? What were we going to do? At that moment I still could not believe what was happening to us. We had been such a strong family unit, doing everything together. Dick knew me better than anyone else. My best friend and love of nineteen years was gone. I knew I had to continue forward but I did not know how I was going do it. Still, I had other things I had to concentrate on right now.

Dick and I had previously expressed our wishes for burial at an impromptu discussion about obituaries at the dinner table one summer night in Virginia Beach. Our surprise and overwhelming attitude toward Dick's sister, Vicki (when she brought up the subject of writing an obituary ahead of time so your loved ones would not have the task) now seemed ridiculous. We did not write our obituaries then, but we did discuss our final wishes to be cremated. I was reassured that I was following my husband's wishes. Thank you, Vicki. I learned that death is something we need to discuss. Once we reach our adult life, each of us should express our final wishes to our loved ones. It is an important part of life to have our final wishes known, so our loved ones can carry them out without hesitation.

"And I pray that Christ will be more and more at home in your hearts as you trust in Him. May your roots go down deep into the soil of God's marvelous love. And may you have the power to understand, as all God's people should, how wide, how long, how high, and how deep his love really is. May you experience the love of Christ though it is so great you will never fully understand it. Then you will be filled with the fullness of life and power that comes from God."

Ephesians 4:17-19

✝

We were surrounded with so much love support and caring from our family, church, friends, and co-workers. I can't describe it in words. God knew we would be taken care of.

We traveled the thirty miles to the funeral home for the traditional visitation we have each attended at one time or another. The only difference was this was for my husband, my children's father. I wasn't sure if there was a protocol for me to follow. I was numb inside as I managed to get through the evening. I really don't remember much of anything. I look back and to this day, it is all such a blur. I was overwhelmed by the number of people who were there to share in our grief. They were offering to help me with everything. I do remember that the Lions Club members were there to quietly pay their respects. They had lost a dear friend and grieved deeply.

Lew and Georgeann Kinney from our church were there. They had become friends with Dick soon after we moved to Centerburg. At first I did not know them as well as Dick did, but we became good friends almost immediately. After all, I had never met a person with the same name as myself. Lew approached me the evening of the visitation to let me know to contact him if I needed anything.

He emphasized "anything". What a kind and generous thing for him to say. I could not imagine what I would need, but God knew. He would bring us together very soon. I had no idea how Lew and Georgeann would become such and important part of Katie, Richard and my lives and how they would put their lives on hold to help us through this devastating tragedy. God put them in our lives for a reason. I know that now and I am forever grateful for their continued love and friendship.

At our church the next morning, we slowly entered the sanctuary for a short visitation time before Dick's funeral. My brother David put his hand on my shoulder and said "Do you feel it?" He turned to my brother Robert who was walking behind him and asked "Can you feel it?" David said now I know what Dick was talking about. God's presence was so strong. Their knees became weak. They were overwhelmed and could only describe it as a love so powerful. I smiled. I knew exactly what they were feeling. "And I pray that Christ will be more and more at home in your hearts as you trust in Him. May your roots go down deep into the soil of God's marvelous love. And may you have the power to understand, as all God's people should, how wide, how long, how high, and how deep his love really is. May you experience the love of Christ though it is so great you will never fully understand it. Then you will be filled with the fullness of life and power that comes from God." Ephesians 4:17-19

We proceeded with the idle motions of the day. Over 200 people crowded into the pews for the funeral, which was a celebration of Dick's short life and a lasting comfort to the family. The meal prepared for all of us by my church families' loving and caring hands and the respect and reverence shown to us by everyone will never be forgotten.

My parents stayed with Katie, Richard and I for several weeks. The rest of the family had to return home. It was especially sad saying goodbye to Pat and LP, Wanda, Vicki and Terry. They had lost a son and a brother they deeply loved. It was difficult for Katie, Richard and I to go on with our lives because Dick was everywhere -- our church, our home, the roads we traveled together, the golf course I passed each day.

The Lions Club members planned to plant a tree in Dick's memory on that golf course. At the tree planting ceremony, I handed a fellow Lions Club member a tin of Dick's ashes. As I walked toward the 9th fairway to join the friends already gathered to take part in this solemn occasion. I looked back to see him respectfully put Dick's ashes on the seat of the golf cart. As we stood in a circle around the tree being planted, we watched with a smile as the golf cart approached with Dick's ashes sitting on the passenger's seat. How fitting! His ashes were quietly buried under the tree as each person said their last goodbye. The tree can be seen from the main road we traveled each day we lived in Centerburg. Each day as I was driving toward Columbus, I would always turn to catch a glimpse of the beautiful pine tree. Memories flooded my mind as I prayed for the emptiness and pain to subside.

"Dear brothers and sisters, whenever trouble comes your way, let it be an opportunity for joy. For when your faith is tested, your endurance has a chance to grow. So let it grow, for when your endurance is fully developed, you will be strong in character and ready for anything".

James 1:2-4

✝

One is not prepared for the overwhelming grief. It consumes every waking moment and your dreams too. You are constantly reminded of how your life will never be the same again. The empty chair at the dinner table. The empty bed. Nighttime was the loneliest because that was the time reserved just for the two of us. It did not matter what had happened during the course of our day, I knew Dick would be there beside me as we worked through our daily life and made plans for our future. Now I was alone and the sole provider for two children. I would finally fall asleep, only to be awakened with tears in my eyes from a dream I had that Dick had died. I awakened to reach out for him only to realize it was not a dream. Dick was gone from this earth forever. There was no escaping the grief I was feeling.

The most comforting place, our church, a place of refuge, became a place of sadness and loneliness. It took several months before I could actually walk into the church sanctuary alone. Sit in a pew for Sunday service alone. Although I was surrounded by church family, it was not the same. Everyone deals with loss in their own way and their own time. Eventually you do learn how to cope each day without your loved one in your life. You learn what to do to avoid triggering those unexpected emotions.

I completed the legal paper work necessary when you lose a spouse, and I finally realized that returning to work and school would be a much needed distraction. I found it very difficult to get out of bed each morning. If it had not been for my children, I am sure I would have stayed right there. Each day you keep on going because you have to for the children, but eventually you keep on going because you want to. Katie, Richard and I knew we had to resume some normalcy, whatever that might be. Everyone wanted to comfort us but I could tell they did not know what to say. It was awkward for them.

Instead, I found myself comforting everyone around me. I knew two of the young parents in my after school program were widowed a couple of years earlier. They helped me through some difficult times. I questioned if what I was feeling was normal --the feeling that I was not going to make it through life without my husband and watching my children live without their father. That pain was most difficult because it was a pain I knew would last forever. I was unable to shelter Katie and Richard from the pain of losing their father. They both reassured me that what I was feeling was normal and we would learn to cope day to day. Not until I returned to work and spoke to them did I have a true understanding of what they were going through with their life struggles. They were younger than I was with children younger than Katie and Richard. We had a bond now that only we understood. Thank you, Becky and Teresa, for your compassion and thoughtfulness.

Katie and Richard returned to school and my parents reluctantly returned home to Snowshoe Mountain, West Virginia. I soon resented becoming both mom and dad. This was not the way I planned my life. My grief turned to anger. I blamed God for everything. He could have healed Dick. WHY DIDN'T HE? My faith was definitely being tested. Although we place our faith in God, it does not mean that we are immune to hardship. James tells us we should not pretend to be happy about our pain but to have a positive outlook. We should turn our hardships into times of learning. "Dear brothers and sisters, whenever trouble comes your way, let it be an opportunity for joy. For when your faith is tested, your endurance has a chance to grow. So let it grow, for when your endurance is fully developed, you will be strong in character and ready for anything". James1:2-4. It would take several more years before I could heed those words and recognize how fully trusting in God would free me from despair.

"But I trust in your unfailing love, I will rejoice because you have rescued me."

Psalm 13:5.

✝

A few weeks after Dick's death, the owner of the house we were renting informed me that he wanted to sell his house and asked if we were interested in buying it. If I was not interested, he would not renew our lease but put the house on the market to sell. I had to make some decisions immediately. I only had five months before our lease would expire. I re-evaluated if we should stay in Centerburg. I was so far away from my work. Would I be too far away from the kids if there was an emergency? Maybe we should move back to the city. The fact that Katie and Richard were not driving yet meant I was needed to transport them everywhere. I did not mind, of course, but everything became complicated. Not one decision was easy. They would both need to make some scheduling changes.

My friends said I could rely on them if we needed help, but I did not want to be known as the friend who was always in distress. I was determined to become as self-sufficient as I possibly could. I was going to be logical and practical with my decision to either stay in Centerburg or move back to Columbus. I was influenced by the fact that I did not want Katie and Richard to change schools. I would not be able to continue being so active in my church if we moved back to Columbus and being close to my church was very important to me. I resented being left alone to deal with all of these decisions. My enemy became fear and doubt that I could not become both mom and dad. I cannot do this alone. If I let my doubt take over, how would that affect Katie and Richard. They did not need for me to fall apart. I had to move forward if we were going to have any life at all.

I was so close to shutting the door on my faith, but God would not give up on me. He knew our pain and gently guided me through each day until I came to fully understand that God was with me. I was not alone. I never was. "But I trust in your unfailing love, I will rejoice because you have rescued me." Psalm 13:5. I became determined to work through this new life we were living. That is exactly what it was -- A New Life. Not a life I was ready to embrace. Katie, Richard and I discussed our fears, just how we were going to get along, and if we should move back to Columbus or stay in Centerburg. We agreed we should stay in Centerburg. I know they wanted to feel safe and secure and I knew it was up to me to provide that security. It was also up to me to make all the decisions now, right or wrong, as I gained knowledge and experience with each new day. It was a defining moment in our lives.

Becoming a single parent was not something I ever imagined when my children were born, but it happened. Your children are the most precious blessing God gives you. "Children are a gift from the Lord; they are a reward from him". Psalm 127:3. I knew I was going to do everything possible for them to have a good life. That did not mean ignoring my well-being but somehow it happened. I found that I did not care about myself as much as I cared for the children. What I did not realize at the time is that they both go hand in hand. To be a good parent you must care for yourself.

Life was difficult for Richard. He just could not accept me as the disciplinarian of the family. I had to set rules. I was not the enforcer of those rules like his dad. I was always a little more relaxed about the necessary discipline in the family. I was the nurturer. Richard and I were in constant battles over every teenage issue you can imagine. It was more difficult because he would not talk about his grief, of not having a father. He had just turned 16. My son desperately needed his dad. Each day became a challenge.

Katie and I were able to talk more. We had our differences but were able to work through them. Katie also missed her dad very much but she was able to openly discuss her frustrations. Because she did not have the same desire to act out her frustrations in a rebellious way, we worked through our differences much easier. I love them both so much. I prayed for guidance each day as I faced our first big challenge of getting a house built.

Not having any family in Ohio, I spent a lot of time on the phone conferring with my parents and siblings. After much discussion, I knew I did not want to buy our rental home. My family offered to help me with building a new home. Where did I start? I immediately decided to show Katie and Richard the property their father and I were interested in. They both loved it. I had never purchased property before. I was going to need some advice from someone I could trust, someone who knew the area. I called Lew and asked him for help. I explained the situation with my rental home and told him I was going to need to accept his offer. Both Lew and Georgeann said they were more than willing to help me. Georgeann mentioned she had property in mind which might be what we were looking for. I said I will look at that property but I also want to show you the parcel of land Katie and Richard and I are interested in. She said, "Fine, we will look at both." Well, if you haven't already guessed, it was the same property. Coincidence? I don't think so. I knew it was where we were supposed to build our home. I knew it was God working His plan for us. It was also the beginning of a true and lasting friendship and of Lew and Georgeann giving everything they could to help us.

This was farmland that was divided into several different parcels. We had our choice because none of the properties had been sold. Lew looked around and walked each property until he decided which one was best. There was a lot to consider, things I knew nothing about. I was so grateful he and Georgeann were there to help me. The property site was beautiful. The view was breath taking. A few days later we gathered at the property site to complete the paperwork with the property owner. It was raining that afternoon, a rather gloomy day, but as soon as the transaction was complete, the sun came out and the most beautiful rainbow formed. At that moment, I knew Dick was smiling down with approval.

A NEW LIFE

†

With the help of my parents, on March 17th 1997 I became the owner of a little over two acres of land. Before we parted ways with Lew, I asked him what to do next, since we did not even have utility poles on my gravel road. The next day before work I drove to the electric company to find out the process to begin getting those electric poles in the ground. I took care of all the paper work and left feeling very good about that one little accomplishment. The electric poles were in the ground the next week. I thought, "My future neighbors will be grateful." I was making progress one step at a time. Now I had to choose a builder. Lew helped me with everything. Decisions were being made and I felt confident that I could do this. I continued to work each day for the after school program. The daily distraction of work and building this house created a welcome change to the never ending grief of not having Dick here with us.

It would be April soon. We celebrated Easter along with Katie's and my birthdays. Dick and my wedding anniversary was April 28th. We would have celebrated nineteen years together, eighteen of those years as husband and wife. That was especially lonely. The first year without your loved one is the most difficult because you have so many firsts without them. God knows how difficult our life can be and He is with us through each struggle we experience. "For I can do everything with the help of Christ who gives me the strength I need." Philippians 4:13.

My attention was directed toward getting the house built. My parents and brother Robert and my sister-in-law Julie helped me financially. This new house was made possible with a lot of support from family and friends. Lew and Georgeann helped me make a lot of important decisions. Lew worked very hard to make sure we were able to move into our new home on schedule. June came quickly. We were out of school for summer break. This gave me the opportunity to focus my attention toward getting the house completed and to teach Katie how to drive. I was patient and calm as she soon became comfortable behind the wheel of an automobile. Thank goodness for country roads and drivers' education. Katie passed her test. My daughter was gaining independence.

We spent the rest of the summer working on the house. I learned a lot about construction as I worked closely with everyone involved. It was the first summer that we did not visit Dick's family in Virginia Beach. We had always spent our vacation there -- we looked forward to our vacations at the beach. We loved being with family but I was not ready to make that first trip without him.

I became very practical with my decision making. I had to be organized and to always be prepared for the unexpected. I was now head of household, as the IRS called me. My faith in God was so evident. I give Him all the praise and glory for my survival. I prayed many times a day for guidance and strength. When working in a public school environment, you must be careful expressing your religious faith. I did not try to influence anyone but most of my co-workers and parents of the sixty plus children in my care knew of my faith. I believe those who were around me each day could sense my faith and how I used it to get through this most difficult time. It was important to me to set an example to everyone around me that I was going to succeed in living my life without my husband. I automatically became more compassionate and understanding to the feelings of others. I felt the need to help those who were experiencing loss or hardship and to let them know of God's love for them.

Summer break was ending and it was time for us to return to school. It was also time for us to move into our new home. We still had a lot of work that needed to be completed but we could do the work while living there. We were looking forward to moving in. I think back now on how pivotal our landlord's decision to sell his house was to our moving forward with our lives. This was a chance for us to start over – a chance to look toward the future with hope that we were going to be survivors. We had so much help with our move from the Lions Club members, my church, friends and family that we were moved in a few short hours.

Both Katie and Richard wanted to find a part time job, as most teenagers do. I did not want to discourage them from working but I knew it would be difficult without their own transportation. We only had one automobile. Katie was beginning her senior year and she wanted to enroll in the work study program, which meant she could leave school at noon to go to her job. Richard was in class all day and would only be able to work after school. I left for work most days at 12:30 p.m. and returned home at 7:00 p.m. I thought we could not work this out but my determined children proved me wrong. Richard is very proficient with computers and was the youngest employee to be hired at our local computer server's office. Not having his driver's license, he would have to rely on friends to get him to work. On work days, his friends would drop him off at work and I would pick him up on my way home. Katie was hired to care for one of my co-worker's children. It worked out because we could drive together to Columbus. Katie and Richard were responsible for working out the details, which they did. We worked together as a team, knowing it was just the three of us now. I know I made a lot of mistakes along the way, but we were living a new life and each decision we made helped us realize we could get through these very difficult times. We became stronger.

My church family knew we wanted to eventually build a garage. Since they wanted to help me construct the garage before winter, they planned a garage raising. I am sure you have heard of barn raisings. Well, this was the same concept, only it would be my garage that was "raised". Donna Coale, our minister Mark's wife, organized everything. Lew helped with that project, too. He donated more time and supplies. Thank you, Lew. The workers came from all over. There were more than fifty men and women working on the garage that chilly fall weekend. The women's circles and other church members supplied the food. It was an unforgettable site. Their hearts were full of love. God's love. What a wonderful thing for us to witness. People who were our close friends and some who did not know us at all gave so much to help us. I thank God for each one of you. We are truly blessed with the love that comes through knowing Christ.

Fall was Dick's and my favorite time of year. It was especially beautiful in the country. The countryside was vibrant with the colors of red, orange, and yellow. The leaves were slowly falling as the cool breeze reminded us that winter was not far way. Dick's birthday was September 27th; he would have been 48 years old. He was so young when he died. We were reminded that life really is short and we need to live each day like it was our last. It sounds cliché but it is so true. You find out what's important in life when tragedy strikes. Don't waste a moment of it.

Thanksgiving would soon be here. We were planning Richard's baptism and his joining in church membership. My parents and Kingston joined us on that special day. I was sitting in church during the sermon when I heard a voice say, "You need to take better care of yourself." I looked around to see who was talking to me when I heard it again. I leaned over to my mother who was sitting next to me and asked in a soft whisper, "What did you say?" She shrugged her shoulders indicating she had not said anything. I let it go until after the church service, then I confided in my mother what I heard while listening to the Sunday sermon. I thought she would think I was being silly. Instead she agreed that I needed to take better care

My Faith and Courage

of myself and continued by discussing how concerned everyone was about my health. I said "I know, and I am going to do better about getting healthy." I had gained a lot of weight and my blood pressure was high. I chose not to see a doctor. The stress of losing a husband, taking care of Katie and Richard, building our home and working was taking a toll and it was evident to everyone but me. Soon I forgot the subtle warning and continued living on the same path of destruction as my life reeled out of control. I slipped away from my Biblical understanding of fully trusting in where God was leading me.

I was not looking forward to Thanksgiving Day. I could not imagine sitting at the dinner table without Dick there. For one moment I thought, "What do I have to be thankful for? My life has been turned upside down and you want me to be thankful?" It was so easy for me to slip back into a deep depression. I could not focus on what we had lost or how difficult it was going to be not to have Dick with us this Thanksgiving. The emotions that were triggered by those thoughts and memories were just too painful. I was jealous of my family and friends whose families were still intact. They did not know what I was going through, thank goodness. It was obvious that I was still angry with life in general. I was gently reminded that I had a lot to be thankful for. Most importantly, I had my two wonderful children and all the people who loved us and were a part of our lives.

My family and friends invited us to share Thanksgiving dinner with them. I knew what they were trying to do. It was very thoughtful. My brother Robert and sister-in-law Julie flew Katie, Richard and me to their home in Boston. They thought a change in tradition might be what we needed. Thank you, Lord, for my wonderful friends and family.

I was already looking ahead to December and thinking about how I was going to get through Richard's birthday and the excitement of Christmas. I was nervous about how I was going to handle it. I could not let my anxious feelings ruin this special time of the year for Katie and Richard and the rest of the family. I decided to be honest with everyone and let them know that if Thanksgiving was any indication of how difficult this time of the year was for me, I was sure Christmas would not be any different. Of course we planned on attending Church, but anything else I wasn't so sure about.

I could not get excited about the upcoming holiday season. I never fully understood what it meant to be depressed during the holidays. I completely understand now. The pain and loneliness this time of the year can bring is indescribable. Please, Linda T., forgive me for not understanding. I hope I was never disrespectful when you were not so eager to join in holiday celebrations with us. I completely understand now. I did not decorate a tree that first Christmas. I could not find the energy to drag any decorations from our basement or plan on any holiday festivities. I have since asked my children for forgiveness.

Walking into a Hallmark store to purchase Christmas cards was one of those moments that completely took me by surprise. I felt I needed to send out cards to let family and friends know we were doing the best we could and to give them our new address, but it definitely did not become a Hallmark moment. My eyes glanced at the "For my Husband" and "To Dad" cards and my heart sank. Katie and Richard always enjoyed picking out the perfect card and we always had to shop for that special gift, usually something to do with golf or bowling. That tradition was gone now. I was jealous of all the women at the Hallmark store picking out cards for their husbands, their children excited to pick out the perfect card with a special message for their dads. I had to exit the store as tears came to my eyes. Dick and I were always exchanging cards for special occasions or for no reason at all, other than just to say I'm thinking of you today. He would surprise Katie and myself with flowers. He would surprise Richard with a new computer game or movie video. His macho exterior was a disguise for his true gentle nature.

We made it through winter. It was beautiful in the country. I enjoyed everything about it. I loved our house. The night sky was so black

My Faith and Courage

that the constellations could be easily identified. It was breathtaking. Living in the country gave me such peace and contentment that my hectic life could be forgotten for a short while. It offered a brief distraction from the loneliness.

February 26th came with the reflection of how we made it through our first year without a husband and father. Thank you, Lord, for helping us through this painful and difficult year. I was gaining wisdom from becoming a widow and the many life changes and experiences that had already occurred.

Winter gave way to spring and then summer. Each season was becoming more beautiful and, of course, bringing more work. Richard wanted to get his driver's license. I agreed it was time. I repeated the same process with Richard that I did for Katie and he soon became a licensed driver. He was still working his computer job and really needed a car. With the help of a dear friend Dan and Richard's Uncle Jerry (my sister Libby's husband), Richard purchased a used car. I wanted him to become more independent, but new worries would follow those first few months as he anxiously took to the road. There were many life lessons we managed to get through. I smile as I think back.

Katie, Richard and I worked together to manage our home and property. At times they resented having to spend afternoons doing chores, but they soon realized we had no choice. We had to work together. The book of Ruth teaches us that when we have experienced God's faithfulness and kindness, we should respond by showing integrity. No matter how devastating our present situation may be, our hope is in God. We tend to think of blessings in terms of prosperity rather than the high quality of relationships God makes possible for us.

The book of Ruth reminded me that the relationships Dick and I made throughout our life were of very high quality. I am grateful to everyone who helped us through this most difficult time. I am still reminded with each visit to my hairdresser Cassie, how in those difficult times she tried to boost my spirit with a new haircut or look. She had been cutting Dick's hair before we met and she was more than the person who gave my children their first hair cuts. She was a good friend. She never pushed me with suggestions. She knew when I was ready. I always left her feeling better than when I walked through her salon door. She and Dan, the shop owner, were always there to comfort and guide me. They took the time to listen and my spirit was always lifted, knowing they truly cared about Richard, Katie and me.

Katie still had the desire to become an elementary school teacher. Her teachers at Marburn Academy always encouraged her to follow her dream. With hard work and lots of studying anything was possible. She did work and study hard. When she transitioned from Marburn Academy into the public school system at Centerburg High School, there were teachers who both encouraged and discouraged her about wanting to go on to college. School was still difficult for her. Bonnie was one teacher who influenced and helped Katie through her transition. Bonnie specialized in learning differences. She was dedicated to her profession and a true educator. She, along with several other teachers, helped Katie continue to make progress toward her dream of attending college. Katie was blessed to have teachers at Marburn Academy and Centerburg High School who dedicated themselves to their profession of teaching. Unfortunately, that was not always the case with every teacher at Centerburg High School and life lessons were learned along the way -- lessons that Katie will keep with her the rest of her life.

During a scheduled parent teacher conference her senior year, I was told by one particular teacher to not expect Katie to attend college. She was not college material. I was offended by this teacher's comments and I knew Katie would be, too. I felt sorry for this teacher's inability to encourage and motivate her students, but she was not going to influence my daughter. I was frustrated because I knew if Dick were here he would put that teacher in her place, but he wasn't here.

I had to step up and defend my daughter's right to continue her education. I politely disagreed with her comments. Once again, I was out of my comfort zone. I was not comfortable speaking out. I did not want to engage in any sort of conflict, but was I actually going to let this teacher discourage my daughter? I somehow managed to let her know my feelings about what she had said was wrong, and I must admit I left the conference feeling proud of how I stood up for what I believed. I was becoming more confident and satisfied with my new found courage.

Dick and I always encouraged Katie and Richard that they could achieve their goals with hard work and perseverance, and I was going to do whatever it took to help them reach those goals. I was not about to share the teacher's comments with Katie. I did ask Katie why she was so adamant to work with children who learned differently. She said she was determined to encourage students of all ages to never give up and to always believe in yourself. I knew Katie was going to do whatever she needed to do to make her dream come true.

After Katie graduated from college, I shared this story with her. Katie's response was one of compassion for all of the students who might have been discouraged by such hurtful words, hoping no one was influenced by the negative teaching techniques she encountered.

Katie would need to apply for student loans and any available grants to attend college. With the help of her guidance counselor Mr. McDavid, I researched grants and student aid possibilities and by the time she graduated from high school, everything was in place for her admission to Columbus State Community College. Katie and I both agreed it would be best for her to begin her studies at a small college. She would major in Early Childhood Development. If she did well, she could graduate with her associate's degree from Columbus State Community College. She would then transfer to Otterbein College, a small, private, liberal arts college in Westerville, Ohio, enroll in their continuing studies program, and study for her Bachelor's Degree in Elementary Education. It was a plan.

Katie set her goals and never looked back. She graduated from high school on June 4, 1999. It was an exciting day and a difficult day because her dad was not there to share in this wonderful accomplishment. All of her grandparents made sure they were there on this special day -- Pat and LP, and George and Margie.

Katie knew she would need to get a full-time job to supplement her financial aid and began working for a licensed child care center soon after her high school graduation. She continued working in the child care field throughout college. Katie made it through her first year of college at Columbus State by studying and working hard. She has an incredible spirit and drive. Katie also took advantage of the college's learning disability program. This gave her the confidence and tools needed to succeed in obtaining her degree. She made a comment when she first started the program: "Mom, the help is there. Why shouldn't I take advantage of it? Just because I learn differently does not mean I can't succeed in college."

We were once again faced with life changing events that would require faith and courage from each of us -- that God was going to get my mother through open heart surgery and that my father would survive a debilitating stroke. Within a couple of months, they both successfully made it though these life setbacks and were well on their way to recovery. Walking into a hospital so soon after Dick's death was difficult, but I knew I had to do it. It confirmed what I already knew. We need to live each day to its fullest.

Richard made it through his senior year at Centerburg High School. He was not as anxious as Katie to continue his education, but he thought he wanted to give college a try. He agreed he would think about taking a few classes at Columbus State in the fall. I researched the same grants and loans for Richard and things were in place if he chose to attend Columbus State. He also considered joining the Navy. Both his father and grandfather had been in the Navy and Pat, Richard's grandmother, retired after 36 years working for the Navy as a civilian Military Pay Director. Richard had learned a lot about the Navy from each of them and his interest in the Navy grew.

His dream was to become a pilot. If not flying for the Navy, then he would fly commercial.

I wanted Richard to be happy with whatever he chose to do. He was so unsettled with life in general. He was acting out with anger and rebellion at losing his father. I was unable to help him through this difficult time. My father preached attitude throughout Richard's junior and senior year of high school and he didn't think it registered at all. He was proudly surprised when he received a "thank you" e-mail from Richard a few years later.

HIS PLAN

✝

Richard's high school graduation ceremony would be held on June 3, 2000. I was preparing for family to arrive the next weekend to share in the celebration. It was May 28, 2000 -- Memorial Day weekend. There was so much I needed to do to get ready for the arrival of family. I spent all day Saturday working outside. It was beautiful and I wanted to take advantage of the nice spring day. Rain was predicted for Sunday and Monday, so I thought I could work inside on those days. I had everything worked out to make the next week less hectic for myself. I tried to be as organized as possible. I wanted to enjoy visiting with everyone. I told Katie and Richard they did not need to help me because I knew graduation parties were going on and I wanted them to enjoy the afternoon and evening with their friends. We could work together on Monday to finish everything I did not get completed. We each had Memorial Day off and could work on the house if we needed to.

Richard went to Parkersburg, West Virginia for the night to attend a good friend's graduation party. Parkersburg was only a few hours away and he reassured me he would be home Sunday afternoon. Katie had plans to attend a party and stay with friends in Columbus for the night. I was going to be alone and frankly did not mind.

By late evening I had accomplished a lot. I was trying to prepare myself for that special day in my son's life when I knew once again we would miss his father not being here. I had one of my usual headaches, but thank goodness it was not a migraine. I thought I would just eat dinner and watch a little TV and go to bed. I was exhausted from working outside all day. I locked the house and turned out all of the lights.

The phone rang around midnight. It was Katie telling me she was on her way home from Columbus. I could hear a lot of noise in the background and realized she was still at the party. I asked her why she was coming home. She said, "I don't know, Mom. I just know I need to be home tonight." My first thought was that something was wrong. She said "nothing is wrong. I am actually having a great time." I tried to discourage her from driving the thirty miles back to Centerburg because it was late; but she would not listen. She was adamant about coming home. My daughter was a responsible young adult and I trusted her decision to drive home. At least she called to let me know she was on her way. She did not want to frighten me by coming home unexpectedly. I told her I would turn the lights back on for her and unlock the door. I asked her to please be careful since it was late and to come back to my bedroom to say goodnight when she arrived home. I could not figure out what was going on.

I stayed awake until Katie walked through the door safe and sound. I don't care how old your children are, you always worry about them. She came into my bedroom to say goodnight and I asked her one more time, "Katie, why did you really come home tonight? You can tell me if something happened." She said, "Mom, nothing happened. I was sitting and talking with my friends when out of nowhere I got the urgent feeling I needed to get home. I have never experienced this feeling before. I tried to ignore it at first. That is why I called you to check to make sure everything was OK at home. When I spoke to you and realized everything was fine, I tried again to ignore the uneasy feeling I was having. I tried to continue having fun with my friends but I could not. I just decided to give into the feelings I was having and made the decision to drive home." I said, "I wonder what that was all about?" Katie said she had no idea. I told her to sleep in, that I would be going to church in the morning and how much I loved her. We hugged each other and said goodnight. Those would be the last words we spoke for the next five days.

A little before 6:00 AM on May 29, 2000, it became evident why she came home. God performed a miracle in my life and started a succession of events that only He could control. My bedroom, the master suite, was located on the main floor of the house. Katie and Richard's bedrooms and bath were upstairs. Katie's bedroom was located directly above mine. Katie awakened to loud banging noise coming from my bedroom area and came running downstairs to find me having a violent seizure on my bathroom floor. She was very frightened and all alone. She could tell I was breathing because I kept saying help me but I would not respond to her questions. There was so much blood all over the bathroom floor. She realized it was coming from my mouth but she did not know why. She knew she had to call 911, which she did. While waiting on the ambulance she frantically called Richard in Parkersburg to explain what was happening and that he needed to get home as fast he could. She called a very close friend, Teresa, who was an RN, but Teresa did not answer her phone. Katie left an urgent message for her stating that she needed help. Not knowing when the ambulance would arrive, she kept trying to find someone who could be with her. She reached a friend from Centerburg who had been with Katie and her friends the previous evening. He immediately came to our house.

At the exact minute the 911 call came through to our local Centerburg EMT, my friend Karen and her husband Mark were preparing to begin their shift. They weren't officially on duty; they still had a few minutes before their shift began. Karen thought about letting the medics already on duty take the call but decided to go ahead and respond. Karen is like that, always thinking of others. She picked up the call and was dispatched to my address. Karen and Mark did not recognize the street number as mine until they got closer to my house.

The dispatcher was not real clear about the problem, which was classified as domestic violence. This confused Karen and Mark because they knew I was living with Katie and Richard. How could it be domestic violence? They did not know what they were going to find. Karen and Mark found me on my bathroom floor, still in the midst of a violent seizure. The vanity doors were torn off the hinges and I had knocked the commode off its base. I was very combative. Karen later told me my strength only complicated their ability to treat me. They determined that I had bitten my tongue almost in half and was barely breathing. Both Karen and Mark new I had a serious brain injury. Not being medical doctors, they could not make the diagnosis of a brain hemorrhage, but they were fairly certain that was what I was having.

They tried to stay cool for Katie. It was a life threatening situation and time was of the essence. Karen said when you answer a call and it's someone you know, you have to separate yourself from the emotional attachment. You want to take the time to comfort and console the loved one who is so scared and standing by, anxiously waiting for a word, an explanation of what's happening, but the job of a paramedic is to stay focused on the patient. Karen explained later that she had to disassociate herself from her emotional state of mind. That was difficult for Karen because she knew it was a real possibility I was going to die and Katie was all alone and like a daughter to her. She and Mark stabilized me.

Their first thought was I needed to be life-flighted to the hospital, but the helicopter was grounded due to weather. It was raining as predicted. They made life-saving decisions for me that morning, which meant that the ambulance was the only way to transport me to the hospital. They were instructed to transport me to our local county hospital which was a little closer, but they both felt if I had any chance of survival. I needed to get to a larger hospital more equipped to handle my injury. As I was being put into the ambulance, Karen turned to Katie and told her they would do everything they could for me. Karen knew it was a real possibility I was not going to make it to the hospital.

The ambulance drove away with sirens blaring and with Katie and her friend following closely. Katie reflected for a moment about coming home the previous evening. She knew it was God who had sent her home. If Katie had not made the choice to come home, I would not be alive today. Doctors determined that I would have died that morning on my bathroom floor without medical attention. Katie said later that she relived her father's death and realized she now could be losing her mother as well. Afterward, Karen said she thought it was a real possibility that Katie and Richard were going to become orphans but God knew it was not my time. God put each person in the right place at the right time for me to survive.

While en route to the hospital, Katie called Lew and Georgeann and another good friend Sharon. She briefly explained what was happening to me and that she desperately needed them. They were leaving for church but instead would meet her at the hospital as soon as possible. The ambulance arrived at the hospital in record time. It was early Sunday morning. No traffic. God even chose the perfect day. I was rushed into the emergency room, and after examination, I was diagnosed with a brain hemorrhage. Karen was right. It did not look very good. I was in critical condition and my brain injury was life threatening.

Karen worked part time in the emergency room at the hospital where I was transported. She knew the doctors and nurses and was able to share important information about me to them. Karen and Mark stayed as long as they could to monitor the situation and to be with Katie. They had to get the ambulance back to Centerburg. Lew, Georgeann and Sharon had not yet arrived at the hospital but Katie let Karen and Mark know that she understood they had to return the ambulance back to the fire house. They were still on duty. As Karen walked toward the door to leave, she turned around one last time to see Katie standing there with tears in her eyes. Her heart was breaking.

Katie was soon joined in the hospital waiting room by our wonderful friends, Lew, Georgeann and Sharon. Teresa was leaving a different hospital after all night duty when she heard Katie's desperate message. She quickly made the decision to find out which hospital I was in route to and would join Katie as soon as she could.

Other friends would be gathering for church soon. Word quickly spread throughout our tiny community that I was being rushed to the hospital, but they did not know my condition or what had happened. As the congregation gathered for Sunday morning worship, prayers began. While Katie waited for more information from the doctors, she called the rest of the family. My parents at Snowshoe Mountain, West Virginia and Pat and LP in Virginia Beach were already planning on arriving for Richard's graduation ceremony on Thursday. They informed Katie they would leave immediately. Katie became responsible for making life-saving decisions concerning my care. Lew and Georgeann helped her make those decisions.

Richard arrived at the hospital and joined Katie in the waiting room as she tried to explain to him what was going on. She did not know much at that time, only that I was in critical condition with a brain hemorrhage. They were both allowed to see me before hospital staff took me away for more extensive tests. I can't imagine what Katie and Richard were going through. The doctors were concerned about any possible brain damage I might have, but they first needed to get my blood pressure lowered. It was dangerously high and the medicines were not working. I was on a respirator and in a medically induced coma with my hands in restraints. This infuriated Richard and this time he had difficulty refraining from letting the nurses know he did not like it. He was immediately reminded of his father and he could not get over the fear that I was going to die, too. Thank God I don't remember any of this. God was so gracious to suppress my memory from anguish and pain. Thankfully, Teresa was there to transpose all the medical terminology. Katie and Richard were now living a nightmare all over again.

Sunday church service ended and friends started to arrive at the hospital. They began to pray for me. Our family arrived late that

My Faith and Courage

evening. Everyone from Centerburg kept vigil. Because everyone was already gathered for Sunday church services when they heard the news, prayer began immediately for me. God was working his plan.

Later, Katie called my program coordinators to inform them I would not be at school on Tuesday and, most likely, I would not be able to complete the last two weeks of school. She explained what was happening to me. They were understanding and told Katie not to worry. They quickly spread the word to all of my co-workers and began to handle everything at my school site. All were aware that Katie and Richard had lost their father three years earlier and were concerned not only for me, but for Katie and Richard, too. God was with us. We were surrounded by so many loving and caring people.

The next five days were critical. The hospital realized I had a dislocated shoulder and my shoulder would need to be set. I was improving enough for them to remove the respirator. I awakened Friday afternoon with no brain damage and questioned what had happened to me. Once it was explained to me that I almost died, I was in complete denial of the seriousness of surviving a brain hemorrhage. My right arm was in a sling and I was in a lot of pain. Everyone said I was fortunate to be alive. I was not so sure I agreed, but I remembered the Sunday church service when I heard the Voice telling me I needed to take better care of myself. I now realized God was warning me, but I foolishly chose not to listen to Him. God gave me a second chance at life.

It would not be until sometime later that I wanted to try to understand what God had planned for my life. My first thought was that He knew Katie and Richard needed me, but I also felt there was more. God knew I was going to struggle with having survived the brain hemorrhage. He was so patient with me.

I was unable to attend Richard's graduation. Aunt Mary, my mother's sister, stayed with me that afternoon in the hospital while everyone else attended his graduation ceremony. I could not believe

I was not going to see my son graduate, which meant that he would be without both parents on his graduation day, but that was the way it had to be. He did have his sister, both sets of grandparents, his Uncle Robert and cousin Ryan. His Uncle Allen, my Aunt Mary's husband, was there, too.

I came home the following Tuesday. Although I did not have any brain damage, I was extremely weak. It was explained to me that my body had been severely traumatized and it would take some time to regain my strength and mobility. My dislocated right shoulder was a painful injury and it would take longer to heal due to the extent of damage to my shoulder and the length of time before it was actually set. Once the family knew I was out of danger, they returned to their busy lives. My parents stayed with us because I could not drive, and I was scheduled for therapy three times a week for the next six weeks. I was in so much pain that sleeping was impossible. I am right handed and had completely lost all use of my right arm. I did not return to school those last two weeks but I was reassured I could start school in the fall as usual. I would have the next eleven weeks to recuperate and regain the use of my right arm. I became anxious with the thought of not being able to do what was necessary to be able to return to school. My job was physical, mobility was very important. I asked again, "Why me, Lord?" I was not even thankful that I survived this usually fatal attack.

A couple of weeks passed and I was experiencing so much pain and self-pity that I asked Katie why she did not let me die on that bathroom floor. It was a way out of this miserable life. Katie looked directly in my eyes and immediately said, "That is the most selfish thing you have ever said. How dare you? You don't want to live for Richard and me?" She turned from me with tears in her eyes. What was wrong with me? How could I say something so hurtful? I loved my children so much. I knew she and Richard needed me. I also realized that I had to pull myself together. I presented myself as a person who was always in control and fairly together. I was going to get through this but first, I knew I needed to start taking better care of myself. I asked Katie to please forgive me.

I turned to God and told Him I could not do this alone. I needed His help. I realized I needed to stop trying to control my life. "Let go and let God" was a phrase my friends would say. I chose to do that very thing. Everyone kept reminding me that I had survived for a reason. The summer was filled with trips to physical therapy and learning how to use my left arm more and my right arm again. Each day I became stronger. My parents returned to Snowshoe Mountain.

Once again my family, friends and church surrounded us with so much love, but becoming stronger did not lead to the confidence that I was going to be well enough to return to work. I learned to drive with one arm and told my program coordinator that if it was ok with them, I would start school even though I was not back to 100%. They were all very patient. Thank you for your confidence in me. I was beginning my tenth year at the after school program and my site always had a full enrollment with a waiting list. Most of my same students and parents were returning to the program for the 2000-2001 school year. They were aware of my brain hemorrhage and glad to see me back at school. Returning to school was the best thing for me. I was surrounded each day by children, parents, and co-workers who were so caring and thoughtful concerning my recovery.

As I often reflected back on how I survived the usually fatal brain hemorrhage, I kept focusing on the fact that if Katie had not come home that night, I would not be alive and here to write about my story of survival. There is no other explanation. God sent Katie home to be there to save my life. Without her, I would have died on my bathroom floor. Such a momentous event changes a person's perspective on life. It definitely changed mine. I am more grateful for each day that I have here on earth and I hope I have a better understanding of what is important. Not remembering anything after Katie came into my bedroom to say goodnight has haunted me to this day. I have questions that no one can answer. I lost five full days of my life. There is no memory of what happened to me. It's a feeling I can't describe. I was once again reminded that life can change in an instant. My perspective on death changed. My family finds it sometimes difficult to listen to my candid reasoning about why I am not frightened by the thought of death, but the reality is that death comes to each of us. Live life to the fullest with no regrets.

"Or don't you know that your body is the temple of the Holy Spirit, who lives in you and was given to you by God? You do not belong to yourself, for God bought you with a high price. So you must honor God with your body."

Corinthians 6:19

✝

Katie was beginning her fifth quarter at Columbus State Community College and Richard was beginning his first. I was back at work becoming more active in church and going out to dinner with my good friends Merry and Linda. We had a dinner group of co-workers who tried to meet for dinner once a month. I cherished their friendship. I was taking care of the house and actually doing well except for one thing -- I was still not taking care of myself. My blood pressure was controlled with medication but that did not give me the privilege to continue to abuse my body with no exercise, unhealthy eating and a great deal of stress. I took better care of my house than I did of myself. I promised God and myself that I would do better. My intentions were good but I kept making excuses.

I needed to find a plan that would teach me proper nutrition. I found such a program and got the phone number, but I still hesitated to make the call. I laid the number just out of sight on my night stand. It was a nagging reminder of what I had to do. I cried out again to God for help. I said, "Ok, Lord, you got me this far and I am ready to get healthy." "Or don't you know that your body is the temple of the Holy Spirit, who lives in you and was given to you by God? You do not belong to yourself, for God bought you with a high price. So you must honor God with your body." 1 Corinthians 6:19.

The next morning our church newsletter arrived in the mail. On the front cover was a poem written by Samuel F. Pugh. I read "For A Day Of My Life", not recognizing the author's name at the time but I have since become very familiar with his work. As I read the composition, I knew it was no accident that I received this message. I just new in my heart this was a message from God. I understood what His will was for me. The poem read:

For A Day Of My Life

This is the beginning of a new day.
God has given me this day
to use as I will.

I can waste it, or use it for good,
But what I do today is important
because I am exchanging
a day of my life for it

When tomorrow comes
This day will be gone forever,
Leaving behind in its place
Something that I have traded for it.

I want it to be a gain
and not a loss,
Good and not evil,
Success and not failure,
In order that I shall not regret
The price that I paid for it.

I said, "Ok, Lord, I hear you and it's time I made that call." That decision would set me on the path to success in losing 85 pounds. The next year was spent learning about proper nutrition. I gave up my addiction to sugar and caffeine immediately. I had the determination and drive to succeed with changing my life. My exercise of choice was walking two miles a day. I embarked on this journey with a positive attitude. I was ready to begin my new life with a renewed optimism about my future. Katie and Richard embraced the change, as did my friends. Linda and Merry especially encouraged me each day. I was determined to change my life. I know it was my faith that kept me focused.

"Don't worry about anything; instead, pray about everything. Tell God what you need and thank Him for all He has done. If you do this, you will experience God's peace, which is far more wonderful than the human mind can understand. His peace will guard your hearts and minds as you live in Christ Jesus."

Philippians 4:6-7.

†

Richard and Katie were attending Columbus State. They were both living at home. Katie was doing well in school and working, but Richard questioned his choice of beginning college in September. I could tell he was restless and not happy. They both finished the winter quarter as we prepared for another holiday season.

That year Katie and Richard secretly decided we were going to have a Christmas tree. They found the decorations in our basement and while I was sleeping quietly, they decorated the Christmas tree they purchased with the money they made from their part-time jobs. They were unsure what my reaction would be. They were so excited and quite pleased with their efforts and could not wait til morning. It would be three years since we decorated a tree in our home, so they awakened me with an excitement that is usually reserved for the younger children on Christmas morning. They asked me to go into our living room because they had a surprise for me. Groggy from being awakened from a deep sleep, I thought what could it be? I walked into the living room to find a beautiful Christmas tree lit with bright white lights and all of our treasured family ornaments. It was the most beautiful tree I had ever seen. They were concerned that they may not have decorated it the way I always did. I stood there and cried as I held them tight. How thoughtful. I love them both so much. They said, "Mom, Dad would want us to get back to living again. We can be happy; it's just going to be different." My beautiful and insightful children. One moment in time I will always remember. Another life lesson my children would teach me.

We made it through the holidays and we were looking forward to the future. I was feeling much better. It's amazing how getting healthy and taking care of yourself can change your attitude about everything. Little did I know that soon I would be dealing with another change in our lives.

Richard wanted to leave school and move to Virginia Beach to live with his grandparents Pat and LP. He was not happy living here in Centerburg. I agreed that moving would be best, but first he needed to work things out with his grandparents. It was 2002 and we had managed to make it through many life changes. We would get through this also.

Within days, Richard packed his belongings and headed east to Virginia Beach. My heart was breaking, as I watched him drive down our long driveway and onto the dirt road not knowing what the future would hold for him. I turned and looked out over the countryside with deep sadness. Katie and I were left with the feeling that we were all alone and that we needed the one person who was so strong to just put his arms around us and tell us everything was going to be alright. My son was moving forward with his life, but Dick was not here and we had to get through this on our own. I knew it was the right decision for Richard to move to Virginia Beach, but that did not make it hurt any less. He needed the guidance of his Grandfather and Grandmother Goodwin. He would be living in the house where his father grew up -- the house we visited each summer -- times spent together with family going to the beach.

Katie was four months old when she took her first trip to the beach and Richard was nine months old when he experienced the ocean waves lapping at his tiny feet. Their dad taught both of them to swim before they were two years old. They were never afraid of the water. Richard and Katie always looked forward to fishing and crabbing off the Lynnhaven fishing pier. The pier was over 1300 feet long and open 24 hours. We were able to look out over the Chesapeake Bay as far as the eye could see. It was beautiful as the sun set. The ocean breeze brought a chill to the air as Katie and Richard wrapped themselves in their beach towels. At night the lights from the Chesapeake Bay Bride glistened in the far distance.

I went along to watch them prepare the crab nets and to watch their dad teach them just how to use raw chicken to bait the crabs. Dick would juggle between checking the fishing lines he had just cast over the side of the pier and helping the kids manage their crab pots. The net pots were the best to use and Katie and Richard finally mastered casting their nets over the side of the pier railing by themselves. When it was time to check to see if they had netted any crabs, they anxiously looked over the railing as they pulled their pots to the surface. It was so exciting watching them as they tried to remove the crabs from the net without getting pinched. When they were young, their dad helped with that process. They scrambled to gather the crabs for the cooler as the crabs tried to hurriedly crawl away. Katie and Richard would have a contest to see who could net the most crabs. It was one of the few times they could stay awake all night to watch the sunrise over the ocean waters.

We would then hurry home to awaken Grandma Pat with the catch of the day. No matter how tired she was, she would always start a big pot of water boiling as she and Dick began the process of cleaning the fish and crabs. The kids collapsed from exhaustion and headed straight to bed. Family would gather that evening for dinner to enjoy the fresh fish, usually spot and croaker, and of course crab. They listened as Katie and Richard told stories of their all night adventure on the pier.

That house was full of wonderful childhood memories for Richard and now it was going to become his home. Living in Virginia Beach was a constant reminder of all of the great times he and his dad had together. It took some adjusting as Pat and LP tried to help him find his way during this uncertain time. Richard could not figure out what he wanted to do. He was still interested in joining the Navy and following in his father's and Grandfather Hendren's footsteps.

After a couple of unsuccessful attempts to find a good job, he called to tell me he enlisted in the Navy for six years and he would be leaving for boot camp in April. I was torn between knowing it was most likely the right thing for him to do but concerned because of the war. What had he done? I wanted to be positive about his choice to join the Navy. I was proud of him for wanting to protect our country, but realizing that eventually he would be deployed to a war zone gave me reason for concern. "Don't worry about anything; instead, pray about everything. Tell God what you need and thank Him for all He has done. If you do this, you will experience God's peace, which is far more wonderful than the human mind can understand. His peace will guard your hearts and minds as you live in Christ Jesus." Philippians 4:6-7.

Richard left for boot camp on April 24, 2002. Katie and I carried on with our life in Centerburg. Managing a little over two acres, the house and everything that is involved became a little overwhelming without the strength Richard always provided. We both adjusted and successfully learned how to drive the lawn tractor, fix a flat tire, carry 80 pound bags of salt for our water softener and clear snow from our 225 foot driveway. We learned what to do when I forgot to call to order propane for our heating system. Shivering and cuddling together on a cold winter night, we laughed and cried and gave each other a pat on the back knowing we could get through about anything. We missed Richard. It was difficult for us to not be able to communicate with him. He would be away for more than six weeks before we would actually be permitted to talk to him or see him. I thought that would be very difficult to deal with and it was, but soon he would graduate from Navy boot camp. I was still working each day for the after school program and managing the house. Katie was on target for graduation from Columbus State Community College in December. She was still working for the child care center and taking babysitting jobs when she had the opportunity.

I was getting involved in Bible Study small groups through my church. My sisters in Christ, Janet, Emilie, Taffy and Sharon became an important part of my spiritual journey. They were gracious and patient as I moved forward with my studies. I wanted to surround myself with friends who shared in the same desire to learn more of God's word and would not be judgmental of my true lack of knowledge at that time. I was still a baby in my walk with Christ. I was thirsting for knowledge and eager to learn. I prayed that I would become more of the person He wanted me to be. I work on that each and every day. I still have so much to learn.

Richard graduated from Navy Boot Camp in Great Lakes, Illinois on June 23, 2002. It was decided that Katie and I would make the trip to Chicago to be present for this joyous occasion. What a privilege it was to be invited to witness this display of true patriotism. Katie and I had no idea what to expect. We were unsure of the protocol during this special event.

I can't remember a time I felt more proud of my son. I was overwhelmed with pride as he, dressed in his crisp white uniform, marched the regimented formations they had so diligently practiced. Katie and I sat there watching this incredible sight with tears in our eyes. He was not the same young man that left Centerburg six months prior to this day. His handsome, six foot frame portrayed a man with conviction and purpose, fit and strong. His dad would have been so proud knowing he was following in his footsteps. He later told me he was thinking the same thing as he stood at attention during the two hour ceremony. The change in his demeanor was impressive.

The weekend passed quickly as we enjoyed visiting with Richard and hearing all about his different experiences throughout boot camp. Richard was on liberty for the weekend so we decided to sightsee in Chicago. While standing in line at the Sear's Tower, Richard in his dress white uniform was constantly being thanked for his service.

Humbled by the comments, he realized he was beginning a new chapter in his life and this service was just starting.

Katie and I were overwhelmed when a young boy about four years old tugged on Richard's pant leg. Looking down, Richard smiled and said hello. He knelt down to shake the young boys hand as the boy simply said thanks. Richard was surprised by his expression of gratitude. It did not matter if the young boy had been prompted by his parent. Richard realized all ages young and old had been affected by the beginning of the war. He walked with his head held high and proud to be in the Navy.

Our weekend was too short. It was time for Katie and I to go home to Centerburg. Richard was now going to begin his schooling at Great Lakes to become a Fire Controlman, the person who fires the missiles. It was now evident that he would never be back home in Centerburg. Not wanting to say goodbye, we lingered a while engaging in idle conversation. Finally we had to leave, since Richard had to check in at his Navy base.

Katie continued with classes and final preparations for graduation were being made. Remember the teacher who told me Katie was not college material? Katie proved her wrong by graduating from Columbus State Community College with her associate's degree in Early Childhood Development on December 10, 2002. The continuing studies program to which she was transferring at Otterbein College did not require her to graduate with her associate's degree, but Katie was determined to prove she could do it, and she did. She chose not to take a break and immediately enrolled at Otterbein.

Her next goal was to obtain her Bachelors of Science degree in Education. Classes became more difficult as she made the energetic attempt to stay optimistic that she was going to make it. She took one class at a time, one quarter at a time. Her Aunt Libby in North Carolina, a former math teacher, would stay late on the phone tutoring Katie in the math courses she found so difficult. Working outside of school and helping me manage our home were other responsibilities Katie did not take lightly. She helped me maintain our house and property and worked extremely hard to achieve her goal of graduating with her bachelor's degree in education.

Richard completed his schooling at Great Lakes and was soon transferred to Norfolk Naval Base in Norfolk, Virginia. He was returning home to his grandparents Pat and L.P. Although he would not be living with them any longer, he would at least have family close by and would be living in a familiar city. We were hopeful that would not change any time soon and it has not.

My Faith and Courage

†

A couple of years passed as we continued our daily lives. Katie was getting closer to her goal of graduating from Otterbein College and Richard was successfully on his own, preparing for his six month deployment overseas. He was also attending flight school. Getting his pilot's license was a dream for him and he was now pursuing that dream. Flying was his passion. He would complete flight school before he left for overseas duty.

Katie graduated from Otterbein on June 5, 2005 with her Bachelors of Science Degree in Elementary Education. We were all excited that her long journey was complete. I remembered the little girl who had a dream in the third grade of graduating from college and becoming a teacher. As she worked toward her goal, she tackled each challenge with a spirit and determination that she was not going to fail, and she did not. She made the most of a situation, whatever the circumstances. Friends and family celebrated with pride and jubilation, though I had bittersweet feelings. Katie, Richard and I knew this would be the last time the three of us would be together for a while.

Richard received his pilot's license on November 7, 2005, just a few weeks before he was scheduled to leave for the Middle East. What an accomplishment. I was so proud of him. My heart was aching at the thought of him leaving, but I tried not to think about it. Sadly, the daily news constantly reminded us of the war and it was difficult to not dwell on it.

Richard completed his first six month tour in the Middle East. He managed to get through the overwhelming stress and loneliness of being away from home. He e-mailed his Grandfather Dolin while he was out to sea to tell him how he realized now why attitude is so important. He said the deployment changed him dramatically.

Unfortunately, Richard has since returned to the Middle East for a second tour of duty. He is unsure when he will return home. Mailing his first care package at the post office prompted a conversation between me and the gentleman behind the counter. He asked the usual question, "Is your son in the Navy?" I proudly replied yes and said it was his second deployment. He replied, "It doesn't get any easier does it?" I explained how Richard was home for less than a year before leaving again. The postal worker said he was in the Navy and only those who have ever said goodbye to a loved one going off to war know the pain of saying goodbye. I explained how this time was just as difficult as the first. He smiled with a gentle kindness, letting me know he understood how I was feeling. If only I could fast forward to the day Richard's ship pulls in to the Little Creek Pier in Virginia Beach, but I cannot. I will just have to stay strong and pray for his safe return, whenever that might be.

Richard will pursue his plans to return to college to study aviation once he completes his Navy career in April, 2008. His life experiences have taught him so many things. He has matured beyond his years. He now has direction, and a purpose. Katie's own child care center will open in the fall of 2007. She is making her way in a career path where she will impact children's lives with hope and optimism for their future. Through the years she has used her own special brand of drive and determination to find success behind every door she opens. I am so very proud of whom my children have become.

My Faith and Courage

As my children were becoming totally independent of me, I knew I had reached a time in my life where I felt I was being led in a new direction. I was encouraged to share my story with other widows to let them know that you can survive the tragedy of losing a spouse. It does not happen overnight, but in your own time and with your own way of working through the loss. Writing this book has helped me reflect on my journey toward becoming a strong independent woman. I am no longer the same person who married my husband almost thirty years ago. I wonder if he would like the change. I feel confident he would.

I am standing on my own two feet watching as my two wonderful children become the productive adults I prayed for them to be. Not a day goes by that we don't remember their father with a favorite story or memory. It's healthy to remember your loved one with pictures and conversation. It is also ok to still be sad after ten years without that very special person. That hole in your heart will stay with you the rest of your life.

As I reflect back on the past ten years and how we had made it through some very difficult times, I came to understand that it was all due to my faith in God. Four of those years were spent in spiritual growth and praising God for all He had done for me. I responded by serving Him, and reading and following His word. I surrounded myself with friends who were true believers and followers of Jesus Christ.

My friends and family noticed a change in my entire demeanor. I was different. I felt it. Mediocrity was no longer acceptable to me. I found happiness once again. The feeling of hopelessness and sadness were no longer prevalent in my life, although I still desperately missed my husband. The power of the Holy Spirit consumed my entire being. I felt the most content when I was serving God, which I was actively doing through leadership in my church.

I am very secure with who I have become. My friends, especially Linda and Merry, Lew and Georgeann, and my Bible study girls

Janet, Emilie, Taffy, and Sharon gave me the confidence I could do just about anything I wanted to do. As I moved forward without Dick, I was surrounded by many wonderful people constantly lifting me up with encouragement. My life is much richer because of the relationships I have made. What a blessing.

These past ten years have shaped who I am today. I have learned so many things. First, trust in God for everything. Cherish your friends and family and let them know how thankful you are for them and how much you love them and need them. It's ok to ask for help and admit that you are scared. It's not a sign of weakness. Do not take anything for granted. Wealth is not measured by how many material items you have accumulated. Your wealth is measured by the relationships you have made and the way you treat others. Actually possessions mean nothing to me now. I would give up every possession I own just to have one more day with my husband, for my children to have one more day with their father. I also learned that I am stronger than I ever thought I could be. With time, you redefine yourself and gain strength with each decision and accomplishment. It's empowering as you move forward with your life. It's who I am now.

Not a day goes by that Katie, Richard and I don't reflect on our memories of when Dick was living and we cherish those thoughts. We wish we had more time together, but we have successfully worked through our grief. Although our lives have forever changed, we have all found happiness once again. We became survivors.

As I lay my head on my pillow each night, I close my eyes and say, "Thank you, Lord, for this day. It's going to be ok no matter what happens in our lives because You are with us."

I sold our beautiful home in Centerburg and resigned from my job of fifteen years with the after school program to complete this book. I miss my co-workers very much and will carry the memories of the friendships I made with my program parents, children and school staff the rest of my life.

I am now ready to move forward for the first time in thirty years on my own. I have become an independent contractor for after school programming and opened my first site in August, 2007. I am a little scared right now, but excited at the same time. I know I will succeed with whatever I pursue. It's up to me to make this next phase of my life a success. I am determined to use my faith and courage to do just that.

"The Lord will work out his plans for my life, for your faithful love, O Lord, endures forever. Don't abandon me, for you made me."

Psalm 138:8

✝

Dick and Georgann's wedding picture

Georgann's family at her dad's 80th birthday party. Parents: George and Margie Dolin, twin sisters Nancy Pate (left) and Libby Godwin (right) left to right, brothers David Dolin, Robert Dolin, and Georgann.

Dick's family on a Princess Cruise to the Mexican Riviera. Pictured (left to right) sister Vicki Blett, stepfather L.P. Goodwin, sister Wanda Mudge, brother-in-law Larry Blett, and mother Pat Goodwin. Not pictured are step-sister Terry Begley, half-brother and sister Sonya "Dee Dee" and Larry Hendren.

Georgann at Snowshoe Mountain, West Virginia.

Katie and Richard at Snowshoe Mountain.

Richard at Navy Boot Camp graduation with sister Katie. Great Lakes, Illionis.

Katie and Richard after Katie's graduation from Otterbein College, Westerville, Ohio.

Georgann's very good friends. Lew and Georgeann Kinney.

Mark and Karen McCann. The good friends of Georgann's and the paramedics who helped save her life.

Made in the USA
Lexington, KY
23 February 2011